Vladimir Putin

Russia's Autocratic Ruler

John Allen

ReferencePoint Press®

San Diego, CA

About the Author
John Allen is a writer who lives in Oklahoma City.

Picture Credits:
Cover: Free Wind 2014/Shutterstock

5: Ukrinform/Alamy Stock Photo
9: ARCHIVIO GBB/Alamy Stock Photo
12: Pictorial Press Ltd/Alamy Stock Photo
16: Pictorial Press Ltd/Alamy Stock Photo
19: Associated Press
21: Anatoly Zhdanov/ZUMA Press/Newscom
26: REUTERS/Alamy Stock Photo

30: ZUMA Press, Inc./Alamy Stock Photo
33: UPI/Alamy Stock Photo
36: dpa picture alliance/Alamy Stock Photo
39: Rena Schild/Shutterstock
43: ZUMA Press, Inc./Alamy Stock Photo
45: Alamy Stock Photo
49: Maury Aaseng
51: Alamy Stock Photo
55: ZUMA Press, Inc./Alamy Stock Photo

LIBRARY OF CONGRESS CATALOGING-IN-PUBLICATION DATA

Names: Allen, John, 1957- author.
Title: Vladimir Putin : Russia's autocratic ruler / by John Allen.
Other titles: Russia's autocratic ruler
Description: San Diego, CA : ReferencePoint Press, Inc., 2023. | Includes
   bibliographical references and index.
Identifiers: LCCN 2022034322 (print) | LCCN 2022034323 (ebook) | ISBN
   9781678204884 (library binding) | ISBN 9781678204891 (ebook)
Subjects: LCSH: Putin, Vladimir Vladimirovich, 1952---Juvenile literature.
   | Presidents--Russia (Federation)--Biography--Juvenile literature. |
   Russia (Federation)--Politics and government--1991---Juvenile
   literature. | Russia (Federation)--Foreign relations--Juvenile
   literature.
Classification: LCC DK510.766.P87 A66 2023 (print) | LCC DK510.766.P87
   (ebook) | DDC 947.086/2092 [B]--dc23/eng/20220726
LC record available at https://lccn.loc.gov/2022034322
LC ebook record available at https://lccn.loc.gov/2022034323

Contents

A Danger to the World

On April 1, 2022, scenes of a recent massacre shocked viewers worldwide. The images were reminiscent of the worst brutalities of World War II. In the town of Bucha, just outside Kyiv in north-central Ukraine, bodies lay strewn across a road, in yards and alleyways, and at commercial sites. Many victims, their hands tied behind them, had been shot in the back of the head execution style. Some of the corpses were burned beyond recognition. Nearly three hundred were buried in a hastily dug mass grave. Ukrainian troops discovered the bodies, totaling more than one thousand, when they entered Bucha following a monthlong occupation by Russian forces. The Ukrainians found evidence of a torture chamber in a basement beneath a campground. Girls as young as fourteen had been raped by Russian soldiers. When the Russian government claimed that the scenes had been staged by Ukraine, Western reporters who had toured the grim site protested. "I personally saw evidence of war crimes," said CBS News correspondent Debora Patta. "These stories cannot be staged, and the overwhelming grief I have witnessed cannot be manufactured."[1]

Among those who falsely described the Bucha massacre as fake was Vladimir Putin, the president of the Russian Federation and a longtime opponent of the West. It was Putin who had ordered the invasion of Ukraine in the early months

4

of 2022. His willingness to use crushing violence against his supposed enemies—including even threats of nuclear strikes—makes him one of the most dangerous leaders in the world.

Rise from Obscurity

Western experts on the Kremlin—Russia's version of the White House—say that Putin's lies about Bucha, and about Ukraine in general, come naturally to him. As a former agent of the KGB (the Soviet Union's intelligence service), lies, half-truths, and cover stories were his stock-in-trade. "You must understand, he is from the K.G.B, lying is his profession, it is not a sin," says Sylvie Bermann, who served as French ambassador to Moscow from 2017 to 2020. "He is like a mirror, adapting to what he sees, in the way he was trained."[2]

His rough upbringing in Leningrad gave no sign of any special destiny. As a KGB officer posted in Dresden, East Germany, in the late 1980s, he witnessed firsthand the sudden collapse of the

Ukrainian law enforcement place the bodies of civilians killed by Russian occupiers into body bags. The Russian soldiers attempted to burn the bodies to hide their crimes.

Soviet empire. To Putin, the humiliation of his beloved homeland was a disaster of the first order.

Back home in Leningrad, as he rose in the political ranks, he hoped to see a rebirth of Russian power and prestige. Tapped by a circle of oligarchs (or rich business leaders) to replace President Boris Yeltsin, Putin seemed a safe choice to continue a program of halfhearted economic and political reforms. Instead, this quiet former spy proved to be a decisive leader—with a distinct edge of brutality. Soon after winning his first nationwide election as president, Putin ordered a massive bombing campaign to put down an uprising among ethnic Chechens, a Muslim group in the Northern Caucasus mountains to the south of Russia. Photographs of the flattened city of Grozny parallel the recent images of devastation in Ukrainian cities like Mariupol.

Restoring Imperial Russia

Putin has steadily tightened his grip on power. While mouthing support for democracy, he has instead ruled Russia with an iron fist for more than two decades. He has enriched himself and a chosen group of oligarchs with control of Russia's natural resources, especially oil and gas. He has also focused on rebuilding Russia's military. Those who dare protest against his regime risk arrest or harassment. High-profile critics of Putin, from journalists to political foes, have met with untimely deaths, whether by gunshot or poisoning. In recent years, protests against Putin have filled the streets of Moscow and other large cities in Russia. Yet he remains popular with most of the Russian people. News photos of him riding bare chested on horseback present him as a throwback, a romantic figure, more robust than past Soviet leaders and many leaders of Western nations.

Western leaders have struggled to come to grips with Putin's ambitions for Russia. Early in his presidency, he was viewed as a partner for peace and stability. Breaking with the Soviet past, Russia under Putin was included in European economic summits. Politicians from George W. Bush and Barack Obama to German chancellor Angela Merkel have courted Putin as a possible ally, only to have him pursue his own interests instead. When pro-democracy movements sprang up in countries on and around Russia's border, Putin moved swiftly to undermine them. He has accused the West of using such movements to destabilize the region and weaken Russia.

All of this was prelude to Putin's full-scale invasion of Ukraine in 2022. Experts on Russia have noted an unsettling change in his public comments and demeanor. He insists that Ukraine is not a legitimate country and does not deserve to exist. The day after the start of the invasion, Putin referred to the government of Ukrainian president Volodymyr Zelenskyy as filled with drug addicts and neo-Nazis. As leader of a major military and nuclear power, Putin has put the world on edge with his increasingly reckless threats. Some fear that Putin's armies could push farther into eastern Europe. "I've watched and listened to Putin for over 30 years. He has changed," says Michael McFaul, the US ambassador to Russia from 2012 to 2014. "He sounds completely disconnected from reality. He sounds unhinged."[3]

"I've watched and listened to Putin for over 30 years. He has changed. He sounds completely disconnected from reality. He sounds unhinged."[3]

—Michael McFaul, former US ambassador to Russia

Chapter One

From the KGB to the Kremlin

Vladimir Vladimirovich Putin was born in the Soviet city of Leningrad (now St. Petersburg) on October 7, 1952. An only child, he was named for his father, Vladimir Spiridonovich Putin, who worked as a foreman in a metal works factory. Putin's mother, Maria Ivanovna, took odd jobs that she could do at home while caring for their child. Despite the Soviet Union's ban on religion, she had her son secretly baptized as an Orthodox Christian.

In 1952 Leningrad lay mostly in ruins, the result of a punishing siege eight years before by Hitler's Nazi armies. Like their city, Putin's parents still bore the marks of that conflict. Serving in the infantry, his father suffered shrapnel wounds to both his legs and was left with a painful limp. His mother nearly died of starvation during the 872-day siege. Nonetheless, with more than 1 million inhabitants killed in the city's ordeal, the Putins considered themselves lucky to have survived. They shared a rat-infested apartment with two other families on the top floor of a five-story building. "There were hordes of rats in the front entryway," Putin recalls in his official biography. "My friends and I used to chase them around with sticks."[4] But his family were also given certain perks that set them apart, including a telephone, a television, and a dacha (or vacation cottage) outside the city. Apparently, Putin's father was on active reserve for the

KGB as an informer. The Putins took great pride in their nation and its victory over Germany in what Russians call the Great Patriotic War.

A Scrappy Childhood

Putin waged his own personal wars as a child. His classmates remember him as aggressive and always ready for a fight. In the trash-filled courtyard of his apartment building, where the neighborhood kids would gather, he did not hesitate to use his fists when challenged. Although slightly built and younger than most of the street toughs, he never backed down. "If anyone ever insulted him in any way," a friend recalls, "Volodya [Putin's childhood nickname] would immediately jump on the guy, scratch him, bite him, rip his hair out by the clump—do anything at all never to allow anyone to humiliate him in any way."[5]

"If anyone ever insulted him in any way, Volodya [Putin] would immediately jump on the guy, scratch him, bite him, rip his hair out by the clump—do anything at all never to allow anyone to humiliate him in any way."[5]

—A childhood friend of Vladimir Putin's

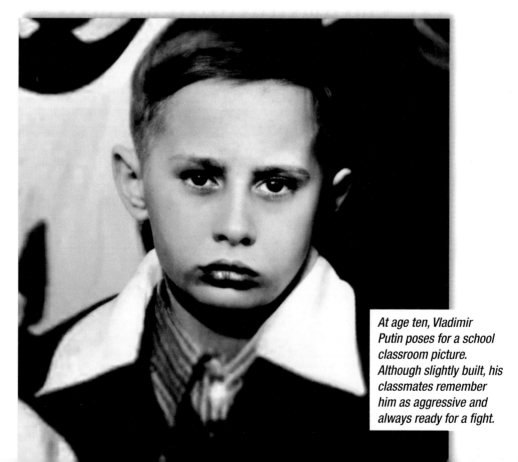

At age ten, Vladimir Putin poses for a school classroom picture. Although slightly built, his classmates remember him as aggressive and always ready for a fight.

At age eleven, Putin began to take martial arts classes to improve his fighting skills. His training was in sambo, a hodgepodge of judo, karate, and wrestling developed by the Red Army. These classes interested him much more than schoolwork, for which he got only mediocre grades. He could also be a discipline problem. When he botched a project in shop class, he got so angry that the teacher had to drag him out by the collar. Forced to sit alone in a corner, young Vladimir repeatedly cursed in frustration. For punishment, the school kept him out of the Young Pioneers, a Communist youth group. He was the only student forbidden to wear the club's bright red kerchief. Later in life, Putin took this rejection as a badge of honor, marking him as a tough guy.

Finally, he began to apply himself, and his grades slowly improved. In his spare time he devoured spy stories. As Putin has admitted to his biographers, he imagined himself as a fearless agent in the KGB, the Soviet intelligence service. He would pursue the regime's hidden enemies and be privy to secrets known only to the most trusted operatives. At the height of the Cold War with the United States and the West, young Vladimir saw himself as defending the Soviet empire.

Putin's Revenge in Chechnya

Vladimir Putin's destruction of the city of Grozny in Chechnya was not the first Russian assault on that tiny Muslim republic. Rebels there had been pushing for independence since 1991 and the collapse of the Soviet Union. In 1994 Russia invaded Chechnya with air strikes and artillery barrages that killed thousands of civilians. Even though the two-year campaign laid waste to many Chechen cities, the rebel fighters held out and eventually won their autonomy, if not full independence.

For Putin, this result was a stain on Russian honor. Three months after becoming Yeltsin's prime minister, Putin ordered bombing raids on rebel positions in Chechnya. This time, the relentless shelling and bombing, especially against the rebel stronghold of Grozny, overwhelmed the Chechens. In March 2000 the now-president Putin, wearing an orange flight suit, flew to Grozny in a Russian fighter jet to celebrate the victory. Thomas de Waal, a former war correspondent, sees the same destructive mindset in Ukraine today. "There are some pretty disturbing parallels," says de Waal. "The use of heavy artillery, the indiscriminate attacking of an urban center. They bring back some pretty terrible memories for those of us who covered the Chechnya war of the 1990s."

Quoted in Greg Myre, "Russia's Wars in Chechnya Offer a Grim Warning of What Could Be in Ukraine," NPR, March 12, 2022. www.npr.org.

Joining the KGB

Despite less-than-stellar marks in school, Putin managed to get accepted to Leningrad State University, one of the most prestigious colleges in the Soviet Union. Even experts on Putin's career are not certain how he managed this. It has been suggested that some Communist Party official must have spotted hidden potential in the young man. At any rate, Putin took advantage of the opportunity. He won the judo championship at Leningrad State while also passing his law courses. One of his law professors, Anatoly Sobchak, offered encouragement to Putin and became his mentor. In 1975 Putin followed the path taken by many law graduates and joined the KGB.

As a beginner assigned to the lower ranks, the new recruit did his share of menial tasks and paper pushing for a few years. He lacked good communication skills for an agent. However, he did meet with success on one important front. He began dating a flight attendant named Lyudmila Ocheretnaya. After a lengthy courtship, the couple were married in 1983.

Soon afterward, Putin was chosen for a yearlong training program for the foreign intelligence corps—the KGB's so-called spy school. There Putin could indulge his childhood fantasies of a life filled with danger and glamor. He felt closer to his ambition of somehow making a difference in the world and changing people's lives. "I was most amazed by how a small force, a single person, really, can accomplish something an entire army cannot," he explained later to his biographers. "A single intelligence officer could rule over the fates of thousands of people. At least, that's how I saw it."[6]

The reality, however, failed to live up to his dream. Posted to Dresden, an industrial city in Communist East Germany, Putin was still far away from the espionage centers in East and West Berlin, where agents would smuggle informants across the border. Instead, he learned to speak fluent German (with a strong Russian accent), drank lots of beer, and put on weight. Not much of a Communist believer himself, he noticed how East Germany's Socialist economy struggled to provide goods for its people. On

Ministerrat der Deutschen Demokratischen Republik
Ministerium für Staatssicherheit

Bezirksverwaltung

Dresden

B 217590 ✳

Putin   Wladimir
Name   Vorname

Pictured is Putin's East German identification card issued while he worked as a KGB agent in 1985. As a KGB agent, Putin could indulge his childhood fantasies of a life filled with danger and glamor.

November 9, 1989, the fall of the Berlin Wall—a concrete barrier erected by East Germany to prevent its citizens from escaping to the West—began the collapse of the Soviet empire. The event struck Putin as a major catastrophe. His calls to Moscow for help were met with silence. "I had the feeling that the country was no more," he recalled a decade later. "It had disappeared. . . . But I wanted something different to rise in its place. And nothing different was proposed. That's what hurt. They just dropped everything and went away."[7] With his wife and two young daughters, he traveled back to Leningrad and an uncertain future.

A Fresh Career in a New Russia

The Soviet Union to which Putin returned in 1990 had changed utterly in his four years away. Mikhail Gorbachev, who had become the nation's new leader in 1985, had embarked on major reforms to the Soviet system. He allowed more openness in journalism, broadcasting, and publishing. He sought to restructure the economy to make it more efficient and productive. Suddenly dissidents, who once had been jailed for criticizing the Soviet government, were able to push for new freedoms. The very people that Putin had been trying to silence in his KGB work now spoke out openly for change. Like many former colleagues in the intelligence service, he struggled to adapt to the new reality.

Over the next few years, Putin bounced from one administrative job to another. In 1991 the Soviet Union collapsed entirely, losing its satellite nations and becoming the Russian Federation. Gorbachev was replaced as national leader by an outspoken legislator named Boris Yeltsin. Declaring Soviet communism dead, Yeltsin hoped to institute democracy and free-market economic reforms.

During this period of turmoil, Putin joined his former law professor, Anatoly Sobchak, in Sobchak's campaign for mayor of St. Petersburg, the renamed city of Leningrad. When Sobchak won, he appointed his protégé to be deputy mayor and head of the Committee for External Relations. St. Petersburg, as a major military-industrial center, provided chances for Putin to meet some of the most powerful figures in the new Russia. He also absorbed the autocratic philosophy of his mentor. He served as Sobchak's "fixer," enforcing unwritten rules and making corrupt businesses pay for their market advantages. Putin resigned from the KGB officially in August 1991. His astonishing rise in Russian political circles had begun.

Meteoric Rise to the Kremlin

In 1996 Sobchak lost his bid for reelection in the mayor's race. Once out of office, Putin moved his family to Moscow, where he soon secured a place as deputy chief of Yeltsin's presidential staff. Putin's official biography is vague about how he accomplished such a remarkable entry to the corridors of power. According to

The Mysterious Death of Anatoly Sobchak

The death of Anatoly Sobchak, Putin's former law professor and mentor, struck Russian journalists as curious. Putin had abruptly sent Sobchak to remote Kaliningrad to campaign for him. While there, Sobchak died from an apparent heart attack. However, local journalists discovered a curious detail about his death. Two separate autopsies had been performed, one in Kaliningrad and another in St. Petersburg by Putin's minister of health. The verdict in each one was a natural death due to a massive heart attack.

Later a journalist named Arkady Vaksberg discovered that Sobchak's two young bodyguards had been treated for mild symptoms of poisoning after Sobchak's death. This was typical of KGB operations, in which underlings would fall ill from the same substance that killed their bosses. Vaksberg theorized that poison had been smeared on the lightbulb of Sobchak's bedside lamp. Turning on the lamp heated the bulb and released the vaporous poison—a trick developed by the KGB.

Sobchak had embarrassed Putin by telling interviewers he would rule like the former Soviet dictator Joseph Stalin. And Putin has boasted of the KGB's capabilities with poison. As for Vaksberg, his car exploded after he published his findings. Luckily for him, he was not inside.

Fiona Hill, a former member of the US National Security Council, and Clifford G. Gaddy, an expert on the Russian economy:

> Like most ambitious people, [Putin] took advantage of the opportunities that presented themselves. Mr. Putin paid close attention to individuals who might further his career. He studied them, strengthened his personal and professional ties to them, did favors for them, and manipulated them. He allowed—even actively encouraged—people to underestimate him even as he maneuvered himself into influential positions and quietly accumulated real power.[8]

In July 1998 Yeltsin promoted Putin to director of the Federal Security Service, or FSB, the successor to the KGB. The promotion showed the growing trust that Yeltsin placed in him. From being a frustrated outsider in Dresden, Putin had worked his way into the Kremlin's inner circle, with access to the regime's most delicate secrets. Barely more than one year later, Yeltsin appointed Putin to be prime minister of Russia. He was now the nation's second-highest-ranked official and reported directly to the president.

Apartment Bombings and a Brutal Reprisal

At the time, Russia was facing an uprising in Chechnya, a Muslim-majority republic close to the Caspian Sea in the northern Caucasus region of eastern Europe. Chechen separatists had been fighting for independence from Russia since 1994. Terrorist violence was among their chief weapons. On September 4, 1999, a car bomb tore through an apartment building that housed Russian border guards in Buynaksk, a city on the border of Chechnya. In the next few days, three more apartment bombings occurred, two of them in Moscow neighborhoods. The terrorist bombings, leaving a total of three hundred people dead, were blamed on Chechen militants. Later investigations, however, would call those findings into question. Mounting evidence pointed to FSB agents as the real culprits in the bombings. They would provide Yeltsin's government, and Putin, with a pretext for decisive action.

As the newly installed prime minister, Putin swore revenge on the rebels in Chechnya. On October 1, 1999, he ordered a full-scale assault, sending thousands of Russian troops into the region. Several days' bombardment by air and artillery left the Chechen city of Grozny in rubble. "[State media] also said then that the military was doing pinpoint strikes, but what kind of pinpoint strikes did we see?" says Russian human rights activist Aleksandr Cherkasov. "[There were] attacks on the center of Grozny, rocket attacks on markets, the post office and [even] maternity hospitals."[9] The world was appalled, but Putin's popularity in

"Mr. Putin paid close attention to individuals who might further his career. He studied them, strengthened his personal and professional ties to them, did favors for them, and manipulated them. He allowed—even actively encouraged—people to underestimate him even as he . . . quietly accumulated real power."[8]

—Fiona Hill and Clifford G. Gaddy, experts on Russia

Russia soared. Most Russians supported their new prime minister's brutally effective methods. Experts have pointed to the Grozny reprisal as the first step to Putin's autocratic future.

An Unlikely New Head of State

By choosing Putin as prime minister, Yeltsin was setting the stage for his own political exit. Overweight, hopelessly alcoholic, riddled with heart problems, and exhausted from navigating Russia's stormy politics, Yeltsin could not continue as president. His attempts to install a Western-style democracy and revitalize the economy had descended into chaos. Corruption was spreading everywhere. Oligarchs aligned with the president were raking in billions from monopolies in natural resources like minerals, oil, and natural gas. Meanwhile, Yeltsin's approval ratings were plummeting. Ordinary Russians blamed him for not delivering on his promises of prosperity and leaving them in many cases worse off than under Soviet rule.

On New Year's Eve, 1999, Yeltsin (right) stepped down as president and named Putin (left) to replace him. It is believed that Yeltsin chose Putin because he would protect Yeltsin from prosecution related to his corrupt dealings.

On New Year's Eve 1999, Yeltsin stepped down as president. He named Vladimir Putin to replace him. It was widely suspected that Yeltsin chose Putin because he trusted Putin to protect him from prosecution related to corrupt deals he oversaw while in office. Sure enough, one of Putin's first acts as president was to give Yeltsin immunity from criminal investigation and protect his papers from possible search and seizure.

> "Russia is a friendly European nation. Stable peace on the continent is a paramount goal for our nation."[10]
>
> —Vladimir Putin, in a speech to the German parliament in 2001

On March 26, 2000, forty-seven-year-old Putin won his first presidential election with 53 percent of the vote. Only one month before, Sobchak had died from a heart attack while campaigning for his protégé in Kaliningrad, a Russian port situated between Poland and Lithuania. Photographers captured Putin's grief at his mentor's funeral a week later. Analysts wondered whether Putin would reject Sobchak's authoritarian ideas in favor of peace and democracy. At any rate, Putin put forward an enlightened vision in his first major European speech. On September 25, 2001, he told the German parliament, "Russia is a friendly European nation. Stable peace on the continent is a paramount goal for our nation."[10]

Chapter Two

Tightening His Grip on Russia

Less than five months into his first term as Russian president, a disaster at sea cast Vladimir Putin in a new light. On August 12, 2000, two large explosions on board the *Kursk* nuclear-powered submarine sent it to the bottom of the Barents Sea in the Arctic Circle. All 118 crew members lost their lives. However, 23 of the sailors had survived the blasts only to die waiting for a rescue. Media reports questioned why Putin did not break off his vacation at a Black Sea resort to address the crisis at once. They also wondered why the Russian government waited four days to seek foreign assistance in rescuing the submarine's crew. While meeting with family members of the crew several days later, Putin lashed out at Russia's independent media. "They are liars," he told the *Kursk* crew's relatives. "The television has people who have been destroying the state for 10 years. They have been thieving money and buying up absolutely everything. Now they're trying to discredit the country so that the army gets even worse."[11]

Controlling the Media

The outburst was uncharacteristic for the usually self-controlled Putin. He hated to have his competence questioned, especially by media types, for whom he had little respect. The *Kursk* disaster ended the new president's honeymoon with the Russian media. Now he went on the attack. Interviewed on state television, he made thinly veiled threats against the moguls Boris Berezovsky, who controlled Channel One, the main state-run television channel, and several large newspapers, and Vladimir Gusinsky, owner of the largest privately run channel. Putin pointed to the moguls' fancy villas on the Mediterranean and how embarrassing it would be should the public find out how they were able to buy them. Within months, Berezovsky was forced to sell his stake in Channel One and ended up fleeing the country. Gusinsky had his channel seized by the government. He was jailed for allegedly stealing $10 million in a privatization scheme but finally escaped overseas.

Putin also took steps to place other media outlets under the influence of the Kremlin. He did not have to send in security police to smash the doors and round up enemy journalists. Instead he employed more subtle means. His staff rewarded friendly media outlets with interviews, scoops, and background information, while opposition outlets were harassed with tax investigations, legal traps, and seizures of documents. Eventually, Putin's political foes in the media got the message. They would either bend to his views or get squeezed out of the business.

According to former Kremlin advisor Gleb Pavlovsky, the *Kursk* disaster altered Putin's approach to the media forever. "After *Kursk*, he changed," says Pavlovsky. "After *Kursk* he started

In 2000, after two onboard explosions, the Russian nuclear submarine Kursk *sank, killing all its crew on board. Media reports questioned why Putin didn't break off his vacation at a Black Sea resort to address the crisis.*

to take very seriously who says what." And, he adds, the Russian media became virtually an arm of the government, whose job was "creating a reality that absolutely doesn't exist."[12]

Brutal Tactics to Deal with Two Hostage Crises

Putin's regime could not hide the continuing problems with Chechen rebels. In October 2002 a group of fifty Chechen militants stormed the Dubrovka Theater in Moscow and took about nine hundred hostages, including the audience members and technicians. The militants demanded a total withdrawal of the Russian military from their homeland of Chechnya. The standoff with authorities went on for three days. About 150 hostages, including women, children, and foreigners, were released the first day. But on the second day, the militants began shooting hostages. Finally, Russian security forces stormed the theater, after first piping in a toxic gas related to the lethal painkiller fentanyl. In the ensuing chaos, the hostage takers were killed, and as many as two hundred hostages also died. Security personnel refused to tell doctors and paramedics on the scene what kind of gas was used, preventing them from possibly saving lives.

Puppets and Politics

Vladimir Putin could not have been pleased when a nationally broadcast comedy show depicted him as a crazed puppet with a blowtorch and a hatchet. The Putin puppet was the star of *Kukly*, a weekly program of wild comedy and political satire during Putin's early years in office. A typical puppet sketch showed Putin choosing his cabinet from a group of politicians dressed as prostitutes in drag. The almost life-size rubber puppets were easy to identify by their exaggerated features and gestures. Not surprisingly, the Putin puppet liked to order people around.

When asked in interviews, Putin insisted he did not mind the sketches. But insiders said the political exposés on Vladimir Gusinsky's network NTV bothered Putin much less than the network's *Kukly* broadcasts. Political analyst Andrei Ryabov said the show was more damaging to Putin's reputation than any criticism from media figures or politicians. Putin's agents in ski masks and camouflage soon raided Gusinsky's NTV offices. Charged with embezzlement, Gusinsky was forced to sell NTV and his stake in a state-run channel. He was jailed for stealing millions, before being released and escaping to Europe. As for the Putin puppet, it disappeared from view—as did the entire *Kukly* show.

In 2002, Chechen militants took nine hundred hostages in the Dubrovka Theater in Moscow. After Russian security forces stormed the theater, the militants were killed and as many as two hundred hostages died in the chaos.

Most Russians approved of Putin's decision to use poison gas to end the standoff. However, families of the victims blamed Putin for the botched rescue attempt. In December 2011 the European Court of Human Rights agreed with them, ordering Russia to pay sixty-four of the relatives $1.7 million in compensation.

On September 1, 2004, almost two years after the Dubrovka attack, a group of thirty-two Chechen terrorists raided a school in the North Ossetian town of Beslan. More than twelve hundred people, many of them schoolchildren, parents, and teachers, were held hostage after gathering to celebrate the first day of classes. Twenty-one hostages were shot on the first day, in an apparent attempt to goad the Kremlin into action. On day two Putin ordered a risky operation to free the hostages. In an all-out assault by security forces, 326 people were killed, including 159 children.

Putin blamed the tragedy and other recent terrorist attacks on lack of centralized political control. He used the Beslan raid as a pretext to extend Moscow's control over the different regions of Russia. In 2000 Putin had divided Russia's republics into seven new federal districts. Three months after Beslan, he scrapped the usual elections in these districts and put his own handpicked people in charge. The supposed goal was to create what Putin called power vertical, or a single chain of command, to strengthen national cohesion, particularly in the fight against terrorism. But the changes also weakened democracy throughout the nation. "It's the beginning of a constitutional coup d'etat [seizure of power]," Sergei Mitrokhin, a former liberal in Russia's parliament, said at the time. "It's a step toward dictatorship. . . . These measures don't have anything to do with the fight against terrorism."[13]

Managing the Oligarchs

Amid all the chaos surrounding his early months in office, Putin focused on a key obstacle to his success as president: the oligarchs. These Yeltsin-aligned robber barons had gotten rich from privatization deals, in which they took over industries that the government had owned under the Soviet system. The oligarchs had thrown their support behind Putin as president because they believed he was an easy touch and would not disrupt their fabulously profitable business empires. However, they soon

A Blueprint for Controlling Elections

Russia's hopes of becoming a stable democracy took a hit with Vladimir Putin's 2004 election victory. That win provided a blueprint for Putin and his United Russia party to manipulate election campaigns and results for years to come. Putin emerged with a system of control that delivered reliable victories for his regime.

Like all autocrats, Putin first sought to eliminate his opposition. When politicians rose to challenge Putin, they were harassed and sometimes even beaten or arrested. Putin also seized control of major news outlets to ensure that his message got out and opposing ones were suppressed. Viewers of state television saw Putin each night dedicating a new World War II monument or opening a new hospital, the very picture of a political winner. According to election analysts Regina Smyth and Sarah Oates, he recruited local government officials, often by threats of firing them, to turn out voters for Putin and his party. His electoral machine created a process for tabulating votes that enabled ballot-box stuffing and fake vote counts. To cap off the election, Putin would promptly declare victory and dismiss any questions about the outcome. As Smyth and Oates observe, "If you want to know what stolen elections look like, look at Russia."

Regina Smyth and Sarah Oates, "Russia's Rigged Elections Look Nothing Like the US Election—They Have Immediate, Unquestioned Results There," *The Conversation,* November 10, 2020. https://the conversation.com.

discovered that the soft-spoken but steely new president had his own ideas. He did not object to the oligarchs' corrupt dealings, but he refused to grant them political influence over him. He made sure they understood who was in charge. According to National Public Radio's Greg Rosalsky:

> Putin offered the oligarchs a deal: bend to my authority, stay out of my way, and you can keep your mansions, superyachts, private jets, and multibillion-dollar corporations (corporations that, just a few years before, had been owned by the Russian government). In the coming years, the oligarchs who reneged on this deal and undermined Putin would be thrown into a Siberian prison or be forced into exile or die in suspicious circumstances. The loyalists who remained—and the new ones who got filthy rich during Putin's long reign—became like ATM machines for the president and his allies.[14]

In his first campaign for the presidency, Putin had echoed the voters' hatred for the oligarchs and their shady sweetheart deals. He promised that the oligarchs, as a class, would not exist under his administration. Nonetheless, most of them thrived. Putin quietly enriched his friends and supporters, jailed or chased away the meddlers in politics, and took a healthy stake for himself by way of kickbacks. In essence, he became the oligarch-in-chief. According to Stanislav Markus, an economics professor at the University of South Carolina who studies Russia's oligarchs, Putin has amassed his own fortune from siphoning off profits from the moguls' businesses. "That's what makes Vladimir Putin one of the wealthiest people on the planet," says Markus. "Nobody knows exactly how wealthy, but that's one of the key processes."[15]

"Putin offered the oligarchs a deal: bend to my authority, stay out of my way, and you can keep your mansions, superyachts, private jets, and multibillion-dollar corporations."[14]

—Greg Rosalsky, of National Public Radio

Showdown with an Oil Tycoon

Some of Putin's battles with oligarchs have played out in public. Such was the case with oil tycoon Mikhail Khodorkovsky. Beginning in the freewheeling 1990s in post-Soviet Russia, Khodorkovsky had leveraged his own businesses, loans from bankers, and money from foreign investors to buy Yukos, a struggling, formerly state-owned oil and gas company. Khodorkovsky streamlined Yukos into an efficient and very profitable enterprise.

In 1999 Yukos engineers made an astounding discovery about an oil field in western Siberia. The field, which Soviet researchers had dismissed as unproductive, actually held more than 5 billion barrels of oil. The unexpected bonanza propelled Yukos into an energy powerhouse. By the time Putin won the presidency, Khodorkovsky had become the richest person in Russia and the world's richest person under age forty.

The sheer size of Yukos and its rapid growth made it a threat to Putin's plans for control. Moreover, unlike other oligarchs, Khodorkovsky announced his intentions to run a clean business. However, he knew this was nearly impossible when dealing with the widespread corruption in the Russian economy.

Khodorkovsky's willingness to raise the issue of corruption led to his downfall. On February 19, 2003, he attended a Kremlin conference on the economy. In front of TV cameras, he described how major Russian officials were making millions from bribes. An embarrassed Putin was shown fidgeting with a pen on live TV. Khodorkovsky's claims showed that Putin's supposed crusade to stop corruption was a fraud. Putin's angry rebuttal sounded hollow, but he would soon have his revenge.

On October 5, 2003, security agents seized Khodorkovsky at gunpoint from a Yukos plane and placed him under arrest. The oil billionaire sat in jail for almost two years awaiting trial. He was finally convicted of tax evasion, money laundering, and embezzlement and was sentenced to ten years in prison. Most of Yukos's assets, including its rich oil fields, were sold off to

Rosneft, a state-owned energy company. The chairman of Rosneft was Putin's deputy chief of staff at the time of Khodorkovsky's arrest.

It was not until December 2013 that Putin released Khodorkovsky. His release, along with that of several other high-profile prisoners, was supposed to deflect international criticism before the 2014 Winter Olympics in Sochi. Living now in London, Khodorkovsky knows that if he returns to Russia, he will face immediate arrest. He compares Putin to a crime boss. "It is the desire of any gangster, mobster type—and that is exactly what Putin is—to intimidate whoever it is that's across from him," says Khodorkovsky. "He wants to show that he's *almost* crazy, that you have no idea what to expect from him."[16]

"It is the desire of any gangster, mobster type—and that is exactly what Putin is—to intimidate whoever it is that's across from him. He wants to show that he's *almost* crazy, that you have no idea what to expect from him."[16]

—Mikhail Khodorkovsky, former oil tycoon

Crushing Any Hopes for Democracy

In 2004 Putin consolidated his power by winning reelection easily, with more than 70 percent of the vote. Although he continued to pay lip service to democracy, he made sure that no serious rivals could emerge. Putin limited the other candidates' access to the press and hamstrung their campaigns with new rules and restrictions. Instead of a competitive election, it became a referendum on Putin's standing with the people. With oil prices high and trade with the West on the rise, the Russian economy was growing rapidly. The worrisome chaos under Yeltsin had been brought under control. A majority of Russians seemed to endorse Putin's strong-arm approach to Chechen terrorists and greedy oligarchs. Nonetheless, many were disheartened by their dashed hopes for democracy. Voting seemed like a sham. "What's the point?" said one manager of a private company. "The system has deprived us of any choice. My refusal to vote is not even a protest. It's just deep disillusionment after the collapse of the democratic forces."[17] Others noted that Putin had stocked his government

In 2004, Putin easily wins reelection and takes the oath of office for four more years as president. He limited the other candidates' access to the press and hamstrung their campaigns with new rules and restrictions.

with former members of the KGB, like himself. The old Soviet-era climate of fear and oppression was making a comeback.

The West's guarded optimism about Putin also began to sour. International watchdog groups questioned the election's fairness. US secretary of state Colin Powell pointed out how the Russian president had limited the press coverage of other candidates. Putin brushed aside these criticisms, suggesting that the United States had had its own election disputes, such as the Bush-Gore vote-count issue. "I believe nobody has the right to think that if they criticize others, that they shouldn't be criticized themselves," he said at a postelection news conference. "In many so-called developed democracies there are also many problems with their own democratic and voting procedures."[18]

Expanding Russian Influence

In December 2005, after warning that political freedom under Putin had suffered a major decline, Russian economic adviser Andrei Illarionov resigned. He also blasted the government's takeover of Yukos and other maneuvers to return the economy to state control.

Yet Putin seemed bent on acquiring even more power and expanding Russian influence in the region. In his state of the union speech on April 24, 2005, he had lamented the breakup of the Soviet Union. "First and foremost it is worth acknowledging that the demise of the Soviet Union was the greatest geopolitical catastrophe of the century," he said. "As for the Russian people, it became a genuine tragedy. Tens of millions of our fellow citizens and countrymen found themselves beyond the fringes of Russian territory."[19] He went on to stress that Russia's place in the world would be defined by its strength. It was an ominous pronouncement. Before long Putin would use this as an excuse to gain territory by force.

> "First and foremost it is worth acknowledging that the demise of the Soviet Union was the greatest geopolitical catastrophe of the century."[19]
>
> —Vladimir Putin, in his 2005 state of the union speech

Chapter Three

Silencing Critics and Maintaining Power

On the afternoon of October 7, 2006, forty-eight-year-old Russian journalist Anna Politkovskaya stepped into the elevator of her Moscow apartment building, intent on getting back to work. Politkovskaya's courageous, pull-no-punches reporting on the war in Chechnya had won her followers worldwide. It had also earned her plenty of enemies. On her way to cover the hostage situation at the Beslan school in 2004, she had been poisoned. Chechen government militias, aligned with the Kremlin, had made threats against her many times. Once, while in the militia's hands, she had been subjected to a mock execution. Her viewpoint on Vladimir Putin was well known. She hated his lies and cynicism and believed that he should be tried as a war criminal for the savagery of his attacks on civilians in Chechnya. Her strong opinions made her a marked woman.

Blows Against a Free Press

When the elevator door opened on the ground floor, Politkovskaya was shot five times at close range. Two of the shots struck her chest and another her forehead, and a Soviet Makarov pistol was left next to her—the calling card of hired assassins. She lay dead in the elevator for some time before a neighbor discovered her body. News of the killing sent shock waves through the Russian news media. Reporters were quick to point out that it had occurred on Putin's birthday. Some speculated that the murder was a kind of gift to the president and a warning to the press. "The result of Anna's death is simple," said Alexei Simonov, head of the Glasnost Defense Foundation. "Every journalist will now practice self-censorship: think thrice, before you write."[20]

The next day Putin arrived in Dresden for a meeting with German chancellor Angela Merkel. As he exited his limousine, protesters began chanting angry slogans and calling him a murderer. Under pressure to respond to Politkovskaya's killing, Merkel raised the issue with Putin at their joint press conference. The Russian president, visibly seething, chose his words carefully. He downplayed Politkovskaya's importance as a journalist but also vowed to bring her killers to justice.

It took eight years and several trials, but finally four Chechens and a Moscow police colonel were found guilty of her murder. Although questions about the case remain, one thing seems certain. Politkovskaya's tireless efforts to expose the Kremlin's brutal treatment of Chechen rebels and civilians cost her her life.

> "I think that in her research [Politkovskaya] reached a point that was no longer pleasant to the Russian leadership, and especially not to the Chechen leadership. I think that's why she was killed."[21]
>
> —Suzana Scholl, an Austrian journalist and friend of Anna Politkovskaya's

"I think that in her research she reached a point that was no longer pleasant to the Russian leadership, and especially not to the Chechen leadership," says Suzana Scholl, an Austrian journalist and friend of Politkovskaya's. "I think that's why she was killed."[21]

A Murder in London

At the time, Politkovskaya was the thirteenth Russian journalist to have been murdered since Putin's election in 2000. Among them was the American-born Paul Klebnikov, who edited the Russian edition of *Forbes* magazine and helped uncover financial and military scandals linked to the Kremlin. In 2004 Klebnikov had been cut down in the street near his Moscow offices with a barrage of bullets. His killer was never found. But the peril for Putin's opponents and critics was just beginning. "I think the problem is not only about Putin but about the people he has been surrounded by," says Andrei Saldatov, one of Russia's best investigative journalists. "They are from the security services, and they tend to see the world in terms of 'threats.' And since 1999 they always believed that journalists are some sort of threat to political stability."[22]

Less than a month after Politkovskaya's murder, another of Putin's most high-profile critics was killed. Aleksandr Litvinenko, age forty-three, was a former FSB officer who had defected to the West and was working as a journalist in London. He had often condemned Vladimir Putin in print, including a book in which he accused Putin and the FSB of planning the 1999 apartment bombings in Russia. Most recently he had blamed Putin for the

In 2006 people lay flowers at a memorial for Russian journalist Anna Politkovskaya. Politkovskaya, an outspoken critic of President Vladimir Putin, was shot dead days earlier at her apartment building in central Moscow.

Putin's Macho Image

In August 2009 Vladimir Putin was photographed riding horseback bare chested while on vacation in southern Siberia. It became an iconic image on the internet, displaying the macho persona he liked to project. Russia's state-run TV, reliably pro-Putin, marveled at his physical fitness. Young women interviewed on the street declared that the president was the kind of man they would like to marry.

It is all part of Putin's ongoing propaganda campaign. He appears taking a dip in icy waters, firing a rifle at a shooting range, wearing a flight suit on a military jet, or communing with nature and exotic animals in the wild. The idea is that Putin is a more vigorous leader than his sober-suited rivals in the West. It is also a reminder to Russians—especially the oligarchs and Russian elite—that Putin is healthy, in command, and not going anywhere for a long time.

death of his trusted friend Anna Politkovskaya. Now he was following leads on a story about Putin's ties to Russian gangsters in Spain. On November 1, 2006, Litvinenko met with some Russians in the bar of the Millennium Hotel, located in London's elegant Mayfair district. A nondrinker, he ordered a cup of green tea and took three or four sips.

Within hours, Litvinenko fell violently ill. His tea contained a rare radioactive isotope called polonium-210. Traces of the substance were later found in one of the hotel's restrooms and all along the killers' path across London. Litvinenko was rushed to the hospital with severe radiation poisoning. He died on November 23. Putin's spokesperson denied any Kremlin involvement.

Litvinenko's murder set off an outraged reaction in the West. For one of Putin's fiercest critics to be poisoned in London, just steps away from the American embassy, seemed especially brazen. In 2016 an official inquiry found that the killing was the work of two former Russian FSB agents. The operation was, in the commission's words, "probably approved by Mr. [Nikolai] Patrushev, then head of the FSB, and also by President Putin."[23] It was an extraordinary statement to make about a foreign leader. But Putin wasted no time showing what he thought of the inquiry's conclusion. He gave one of the accused agents a state medal for services to the motherland. The Kremlin also refused to extradite either man for trial.

Keeping the Levers of Power

In 2008 Putin reached the end of his constitutional limit of two consecutive terms as president. However, he had no intention of giving up power. Instead, he chose Dmitry Medvedev, a corporate lawyer and political activist, to run in his place. In the meantime, Putin would serve as prime minister. Like Putin, Medvedev had taken classes under Anatoly Sobchak, and the two had worked together on Sobchak's staff when he was mayor of Leningrad. Later, Medvedev ran Putin's 2000 presidential campaign and then helped reorganize Gazprom, a huge state-run natural gas firm.

In the 2008 campaign, Medvedev rarely appeared without Putin by his side. Russians had no illusions about what was going on. They knew that a vote for Medvedev meant keeping the levers of power in Putin's hands. After a lackluster campaign, some in the Kremlin feared that voter apathy would hold down turnout numbers at the polls and make the election look illegitimate. Word went out at schools, factories, and hospitals that failure to vote could cost people their jobs. The final tally showed Medvedev winning with 70 percent of the vote, almost exactly Putin's previous total. The victorious candidate vowed to follow the course set by his predecessor. Many urban dwellers in central Moscow were disgusted by the whole process. "It's not pleasant, it's like Soviet times," said one young woman who refused to vote. "They've already decided it all."[24]

Foreign observers held out some hope that Medvedev would prove to be more liberal than Putin, at least in foreign policy. In her first meeting with Medvedev's foreign minister, Hillary Clinton, America's new secretary of state under President Barack Obama, announced a "reset" with Russia. She promoted a new era of better relations, complete with a large red reset button to emphasize the idea. But it soon became obvious that Medvedev, whose public style was awkward and ineffective, had nothing new to offer. A joke circulating at the US embassy in Moscow said that Putin had given his good friend Dmitry a fancy new car—only without a steering wheel.

Russian president Dmitry Medvedev (right) and prime minister Vladimir Putin arrive at a meeting in Europe in 2009. In 2008, Putin reached the end of his constitutional limit as president and chose longtime ally Medvedev to run in his place.

A Prisoner in the Kremlin

In 2011 Putin declared that he would run for a third term as president. Medvedev had accomplished little in four years, other than enriching himself with yachts, vineyards, and country estates. Putin did see to one significant change in the interim. He convinced the Russian parliament to extend the presidential term to six years. Once reelected, he could serve two consecutive terms, meaning he would not have to worry about term limits again until 2024.

Sources in the Kremlin believe Putin had considered letting Medvedev run again in 2012. But recent events such as the Arab Spring in the Middle East, with dictators being toppled and even killed, changed his mind. He did not want to wind up like Libya's Muammar Qaddafi, beaten to death by a mob in the street. As

Edward Lucas, senior editor at the *Economist*, told the PBS program *Frontline*:

> There's never been a good succession model in the Soviet Union or in Russia, and [Putin's] very worried about how he will leave power. He doesn't want to leave in a coffin. He doesn't want to go to a jail cell. He has got so many guilty secrets, so much money's been stolen, so many people have been killed that he doesn't really trust anyone to keep him safe if he steps down from power. So in a way, he's both the master of the Kremlin, but also a prisoner in it.[25]

Facing Down Critics and Protesters

Putin's announcement that he would seek the presidency again, while not surprising, drew some of the most ferocious criticism of his career. In the 2012 campaign, he faced a growing opposition movement and widespread protests. While dismissing the protesters as malcontents, Putin wrote newspaper essays in which he acknowledged certain problems in Russia. These included an economy grown stagnant and in need of modernization, corrupt business practices that scared off foreign investment, and a population that was declining at an alarming rate. Typically, he stressed that these obstacles to development had to be overcome so that Russia would not fall behind the United States and other world powers. He promised to make improvements and offer political reforms. He insisted that his own vision and willpower were what was needed for Russia to achieve its glorious destiny. Many Russians, especially those who could recall the post-Soviet turmoil under Yeltsin, agreed that a strong figure like Putin was necessary for stability. They did not mind his macho posturing, such as riding horseback bare chested. Polls showed Putin's approval ratings at 80 percent, which was borne out by his landslide reelection.

In a video message, Putin linked his victory to support from ordinary Russians. "You showed who the Russian people are, the Russian working man, the worker and the engineer," he said.

From a Boom to a Stagnant Economy

Putin's early years as president saw a significant economic boom in Russia. Rising global oil prices fueled the expansion, and the government ran strong surpluses. Putin took the opportunity to crowd out certain oligarchs like Mikhail Khodorkovsky and confiscate their oil and mineral wealth for himself and his cronies.

In 2008 a worldwide financial crisis caused oil prices to plummet by 80 percent, if only temporarily. The Russian public's view of Putin underwent a change. Although they continued their support, they no longer trusted his economic policies. With savings, stock prices, and standard of living in decline, Putin tried to divert attention from the extended slump. He promised—but did not deliver—political reforms at home, and he summoned patriotic support by sending troops to win small wars in Georgia and Ukraine. In general, Putin has favored political control over economic growth, a choice that has helped him maintain an iron grip on his nation. But experts believe it comes with a steep price. According to Simon Saradzhyan of the Harvard Kennedy School, "What I am pretty confident in is that [Putin's] continued stay in the Kremlin for two more terms, if not more, would bode ill for the long-term stable development of Russia."

Simon Saradzhyan, "16 More Years of Putin: A Promise of Stability That Looks Like Stagnation," Russia Matters, March 13, 2020. www.russiamatters.org.

"You showed that you are a head higher than any layabout, any old windbag. This was for me the biggest present."[26]

Once he had won reelection, however, Putin reverted to his strong-arm tactics. He ridiculed charges of voting fraud—despite one independent monitoring group reporting thirty-five hundred election violations nationwide. He ordered police to break up protests on the street. A crowd of fifteen thousand gathered in Moscow's Pushkin Square to chant "Russia without Putin" and "Putin is a thief!"[27] before the crowd's leaders were shoved into police vans and hauled off.

A Dangerous Enterprise

Opposing Putin continued to be a dangerous enterprise. Boris Nemtsov was a fierce critic of Putin as Boris Yeltsin's deputy prime minister. He specialized in shining a light on corruption, and he condemned Russia's 2014 attacks on eastern Ukraine. In interviews, he had expressed fears that Putin would have him killed. On the night of February 27, 2015, only hours after organizing a rally for Ukraine, Nemtsov was crossing a bridge on foot within sight of the Kremlin. Suddenly, four men jumped out of a white car and opened fire. Nemtsov died on the scene with four gunshot wounds in the back. It was the most blatant assassination yet under Putin's rule. Five Chechens were rounded up and charged with the murder, but questions about who ordered it were left unanswered.

A memorial for Putin opposition leader Boris Nemtsov at the site of his killing in central Moscow in March 2015. Nemtsov was shot dead while walking across a bridge at night near the Kremlin.

As with the killings of other political opponents, Putin denied any involvement and made his usual promises of a thorough investigation. But in May 2015 Vladimir Kara-Murza, Nemtsov's friend and fellow activist, was poisoned. He survived despite falling into a coma and suffering organ failure. Two years later, Kara-Murza again was poisoned and again survived. Kara-Murza blamed the Kremlin not only for Nemtsov's killing but also the attempts on his own life.

Putin's government sometimes employed less violent means to deal with high-profile political foes. In July 2013, just as the blogger and lawyer-activist Alexei Navalny was gaining a groundswell of popular support, Navalny was found guilty of embezzlement in a deal with a state-run lumber operation. Navalny's five-year prison sentence was reduced to a suspended sentence on appeal. However, according to Russian law, his conviction made him ineligible to run for public office, thus removing him as a potential political challenger to Putin.

In 2016 the European Court of Human Rights found that Navalny's trial had been rigged from the start. Added to the corruption Navalny had documented so thoroughly, the trial seemed to confirm his label for the ruling United Russia Party—founded by Vladimir Putin—as the party of crooks and thieves. For Navalny, much worse harassment lay ahead, including a near-fatal poisoning and a lengthy sentence to a remote penal colony. Critics said it was all part of Putin's plan to maintain power. "I think it's important for Putin to demonstrate that he's punishing Navalny," says Nikolai Petrov of the Chatham House policy institute based in London. "If you're leader of the gang, you can't allow anyone to challenge you without being punished and in a way that is a lesson to everyone else."[28]

"I think it's important for Putin to demonstrate that he's punishing Navalny. If you're leader of the gang, you can't allow anyone to challenge you without being punished and in a way that is a lesson to everyone else."[28]

—Nikolai Petrov, of the Chatham House policy institute

Chapter Four

Rising Tensions with the West

On August 1, 2013, Russia granted asylum to an American whistleblower who had been living inside Moscow's Sheremetyevo International Airport for forty days. Edward Snowden, a former intelligence contractor, had revealed the National Security Agency's secret program to gather Americans' phone and internet records. US government officials considered Snowden a traitor and desperately wanted him sent back to America for prosecution. Vladimir Putin treated the case as an immigration matter, of no special importance. But by allowing Snowden to remain in Russia, he knew he was making an embarrassing situation worse for President Obama and his administration. After years of hearing lectures from American officials about human rights violations, Putin relished having the tables turned. His ploy was not lost on US senator John McCain. "Russia's action today is a disgrace and a deliberate effort to embarrass the United States," McCain said. "It is a slap in the face of all Americans. Now is the time to fundamentally rethink our relationship with Putin's Russia."[29]

Repression at Home, Aggression Abroad

But it was Putin who was rethinking his relations with the West. His goal had always been to restore Russia to the heights it had achieved under the Soviet Union. He wanted his nation to be a great power again—the economic, political, and military leader of its region. But he realized this could not be done by copying the United States or the European powers. Russia had its own destiny to follow, and he intended to pursue it in his own way.

Putin's background as a KGB agent had taught him that aggression mixed with subterfuge could keep one's enemies off balance. He continued to rule as an iron-fisted autocrat at home while probing and prodding for advantages in foreign policy. Assured in his mind of at least twelve more years in office, he could afford to play a long game.

Domestically, Putin stressed socially conservative values. He looked to the Russian Orthodox Church as a moral authority and political ally. He rejected social movements such as LGBTQ rights and vowed that same-sex marriage would never be legal in Russia while he was president. He often blamed LGBTQ Russians for the nation's population decline. In 2013, with Putin's support, the Russian parliament outlawed "gay propaganda."[30] The law banned the promotion of nontraditional sexual relations to minors

In 2013 Edward Snowden, a former intelligence contractor, was wanted in the United States for revealing a secret government program that involved tracking personal information. To embarrass the US, Putin granted Snowden asylum in Russia.

and set large fines for violators. LGBTQ activists feared the law would eliminate rallies for gay rights and could even be employed to prosecute those who spoke out in favor of homosexuals. Another proposed bill made it a crime to insult the feelings of religious believers, with a penalty of up to three years in prison if the offense was carried out in a place of worship.

Putin also moved to shut down nongovernmental organizations, viewing them as rabble-rousing groups that only caused dissension. The new law targeted groups with US ties, such as the Peace Corps, Human Rights Watch, and Amnesty International. The organizations were declared a threat to the Russian Federation's constitutional order and state security. Human Rights Watch had condemned Putin's hostility toward LGBTQ rights and warned that it could put gay people in danger.

Putin's approach to foreign policy was linked to his conservative beliefs. For example, in June 2019 he told an interviewer that Western-style liberalism was obsolete. Its values, he said, such as gay rights, multiculturalism, and support for migrants, were in conflict with the majority of the population. He believed they were also a sign of weakness. According to Putin, "Traditional values are more stable and more important for millions of people than this liberal idea, which, in my opinion, is really ceasing to exist."[31]

> "Traditional values are more stable and more important for millions of people than this liberal idea, which, in my opinion, is really ceasing to exist."[31]
>
> —Vladimir Putin

Western leaders such as European Council president Donald Tusk were quick to rebuke his comments. "Whoever claims that liberal democracy is obsolete also claims that freedoms are obsolete, that the rule of law is obsolete and that human rights are obsolete," said Tusk. "What I find obsolete are authoritarianism, personality cults, the rule of oligarchs, even if sometimes they may seem effective."[32] Nonetheless, Putin's beliefs led him to pursue a more aggressive foreign policy. He sought ways to expand Russia's territory and influence. And he defied the United States or any other nation to stop him.

Putin's Friends on the Far Right

Recent photos of Vladimir Putin seated at a long table in the Kremlin, meeting at a distance with some visiting foreign leader, give the impression he is isolated, almost alone. Yet the Russian president actually possesses a surprising number of friends and allies. And not just among the obvious autocrats like himself, such as China's Xi Jinping or Syria's Bashar al-Assad. Certain self-styled democracies in eastern Europe are led by individuals who share many of Putin's views about the modern world.

Chief among these is Hungary's Viktor Orban, who is serving his fourth term as president. Orban touts what he calls illiberal democracy. In practice, that means he controls Hungarian media and the machinery of the state. During election campaigns Orban plays down his admiration for Putin, and he has voted for some EU sanctions on Moscow. But he is also a reliable vote to sabotage stronger actions against Putin's regime.

Another Putin friend and client is Alexander Lukashenko, president of neighboring Belarus. Lukashenko's election in August 2020 was widely seen as fraudulent, and his security police routinely harass protesters in the street. But Putin can count on Belarus as a staging area for his invasion forces.

Coming to the Aid of Ethnic Russians

Putin had begun testing the West's resolve back in August 2008. He sent Russian troops into South Ossetia, a breakaway republic in the nation of Georgia. A former Soviet state, Georgia is located to the south of Russia on the Black Sea. Putin claimed to be aiding South Ossetia's largely Russian population. His real fear, however, was that Georgia's turn toward democracy and the European Union (EU) would influence other border nations to follow its example. Russian tanks and artillery attacked Georgian positions, including cities and towns. The Russian forces were heading for the capital of Tbilisi when President George W. Bush sent US Air Force planes into the area. Only then did Putin back down.

Coming to the rescue of ethnic Russians in nearby countries became Putin's preferred way of justifying his aggression. His stated aim was to bring Russians back into the fold of the Russian Federation. Condoleezza Rice, Bush's secretary of state, noted this idea in all her talks with the Russian president. "He was always obsessed with the 25 million Russians trapped outside Mother

Putin and His Place in History

Following Vladimir Putin's landslide election as Russian president in 2018, members of his inner circle began to notice a change in Putin's outlook. He ruled out any idea that he was slowing down and would probably step down after his fourth term ended in 2024. To dispel any doubts, he approached the day-to-day functions of his office with new energy. "There is a misconception that Putin is tired, needs rest and wants to live the life of a billionaire," said a former minister who spoke often with the president. "But Putin is far from being tired. He is interested in everything and digs into every matter, paying attention to all the details. This is his lifestyle, this is who he is. He can't imagine life without power."

He also obsessed about his own place in Russian history, alongside the influential czars and Soviet leaders of the past. He truly believes that he is destined to lead Russia into a new era of greatness. As part of his program, he has embraced the Russian Orthodox Church and even claimed it had links with Soviet Communism. "And if Russia is God's chosen nation, it follows that Putin is God's chosen leader," says his biographer, Mikhail Zygar. "The president himself naturally subscribes to this view."

Quoted in Mikhail Zygar, "Putin Believes He's Destined to Make Russia Great Again. And He's Just Getting Started," *Time*, March 19, 2018. www.time.com.

Russia by the breakup of the Soviet Union," says Rice. "Again and again he raised this. That is why, for him, the end of the Soviet empire was the greatest catastrophe of the 20th century."[33]

Annexing Crimea in Ukraine

In 2014 Putin followed a similar game plan in Ukraine. Violence had erupted there beginning in November 2013 when Ukraine's pro-Russian president, Viktor Yanukovych, rejected an alliance with the EU, which a majority of Ukrainians wanted. For weeks, angry protesters fought with Ukrainian security police in the streets of major cities. In late February 2014, with dozens dying in the bloody street battles, Yanukovych fled Ukraine. Pro-European groups took over Ukraine's capital of Kyiv.

At that point Putin decided to act. He ordered Russian troops to Ukraine's borders as part of an unplanned military exercise, with fighter jets on high alert. On February 27 soldiers in plain green

> "[Putin] was always obsessed with the 25 million Russians trapped outside Mother Russia by the breakup of the Soviet Union. Again and again he raised this."[33]
>
> —Condoleezza Rice, secretary of state in the George W. Bush administration

uniforms appeared in Crimea, a peninsula in the south of Ukraine with a pro-Russian majority. The soldiers occupied government buildings and checkpoints and captured two airports in Crimea. "Clearly professional soldiers by the way they handled themselves and their weapons, they wore Russian combat fatigues but with no identifying insignia," says Steven Pifer, a foreign policy expert at the Brookings Institution. "Ukrainians called them 'little green men.' President Vladimir Putin at first flatly denied these were Russian soldiers, only to later admit that they were and award commendations to their commanders."[34]

The soldiers' deployment helped rally ethnic Russians and assert Russian control in Crimea. Putin moved quickly to solidify his gains. Following a March referendum riddled with fraud, it was announced that the Crimean people had voted to leave Ukraine. On March 21, despite American and European protests and sanctions, Putin signed into law the annexation of Crimea. Obama and other Western leaders had few options to reverse Putin's takeover. The Kremlin claimed to have rescued Crimea's ethnic Russians from danger, when in fact no danger had existed. But Putin's approval ratings at home skyrocketed due to his audacity in catching the West off guard.

In 2014 Russian soldiers in plain green uniforms occupy an airfield in Crimea, Ukraine. On March 21, despite American and European protests and sanctions, Putin signed into law the annexation of Crimea.

Less than one month later, he authorized another assault on Ukrainian territory. This time his tanks and troops slipped into the eastern Donbas region to support an uprising by pro-Russian separatists. Although Putin denied direct involvement, he was once again coming to the aid of ethnic Russians with military reinforcements. Pitched battles led to more than thirteen thousand deaths, until a 2015 peace deal established an uneasy truce. The Kremlin insisted that Ukraine was historically part of Russia, not a separate country. Ukrainians bitterly disagreed, but their government lacked the means to expel Putin's forces. The West was left in a quandary. As Obama told the *Atlantic* magazine, "The fact is that Ukraine, which is a non-NATO [North Atlantic Treaty Organization] country, is going to be vulnerable to military domination by Russia no matter what we do."[35]

A Muscular Foreign Policy

Putin continued to pursue a muscular foreign policy. On September 28, 2015, he addressed the United Nations General Assembly for the first time in a decade. He chided the United States for meddling in the Middle East and trying to spread democracy by force. The Arab Spring, he said, in which several Middle Eastern nations had overthrown their governments, had produced not democracy but more turmoil and terrorism. "The export of revolutions—this time so-called democratic ones—continues," he said. "Far from learning from others' mistakes, we keep on repeating them. It suffices to look at Middle East and North Africa. . . . Rather than bringing about reform, foreign interference has resulted in . . . violence, poverty, and social disaster."[36] Putin warned the assembly about what he saw as the growing threat from the United States and NATO pushing eastward from Europe. Left unsaid was Putin's fear that democratic uprisings might spread to Russia.

He went on to suggest a broad alliance against terrorism. He urged support for the government of Bashar al-Assad in Syria in its fight against ISIS, or the Islamic State, a deadly terrorist group that was on the march. The United States and Europe considered Assad, who was Russia's staunch ally, to be a murderous dictator and an obstacle to peace.

Putin wasted no time acting on his suggestion in Syria. Starting in the fall of 2015, he launched air strikes supposedly aimed at ISIS and other terrorist groups. But terrorists were not the main targets. Russian bombers also hit rebel strongholds, street markets, courthouses, and hospitals in Aleppo, Binnish, and other cities in northwestern Syria. The widespread attacks caused hundreds of civilian casualties and left millions homeless. An extended assault on Aleppo in 2016 was especially ruthless, reducing the city to rubble. Putin's air strikes went on for months, helping the dictator Assad regain territory and defeat the rebel uprising against his rule.

United Nations investigators later charged Russia with war crimes in Syria, including the killing of children, in its eleven-month campaign of aerial bombardment and shelling. Observers have seen the same brutal pattern unfolding in Ukraine today. "That's

People watch as a civilian building is bombarded in the Al Zbieda district of Aleppo on April 23, 2016. Twenty people were killed and more than fifty were injured. Activists say that Russia is behind the bombardments around the city.

really the sort of case study that we're looking at and getting very worried about, is the artillery tactics that they employed there and this mix of shelling residential areas and then sort of demanding capitulation agreements in single neighborhoods," says Mason Clark, a Russian analyst at the Institute for the Study of War. "It's incredibly damaging and led to untold civilian casualties that they never, frankly, ever really faced any consequences for."[37]

Interference in Foreign Elections

Another part of Putin's aggressive foreign policy was to meddle in elections across Europe and in the United States and Canada. This interference ranged from cyberattacks to disinformation efforts like fake news and scandals. Putin's goal, say experts on Russia, was to undermine people's faith in democracy and government institutions. According to Hannah Thoburn, a research fellow at the Hudson Institute in Washington, DC, "They've been very good at using the West's weaknesses against itself, the open Internet to hack, the free media to sow discord, and to cause people to question the underpinnings of the systems under which they live."[38] The Kremlin dismissed such stories as anti-Russian propaganda.

However, US intelligence officials claimed that Russia had hacked emails from Democratic National Committee servers leading up to the 2016 presidential election. Wikileaks, a whistle-blowing group, published the emails online, leading to embarrassing disclosures for Democrats. Security experts say they believe Putin was personally involved in the hacking scheme. Russia was also found to have purchased thousands of dollars in ads on Facebook and other social media platforms in support of Donald Trump's campaign. As president, Trump was one of several right-wing nationalist politicians in the world with whom Vladimir Putin enjoyed good relations.

Putin had long established himself as a dangerously unpredictable rogue leader on the world stage. He left little doubt that he was willing to take bold risks to further what he saw as Russia's interests. But he was soon to embark on an operation that would unsettle not only his own region but the entire world.

Chapter Five

Invading Ukraine

In 2014 Ukraine signed an historic political pact with the twenty-eight nations of the EU. Three years later Ukraine agreed to stronger economic ties with the EU, including free trade and visa-free travel. These agreements marked a major setback for Vladimir Putin in his ongoing tug-of-war with the EU over Ukraine. Early in his presidency, Putin had insisted that Ukraine was not an independent nation but rather a territory that historically belonged to Russia. He had already poached Crimea, and his forces continued to gain ground in the eastern Donbas region. He claimed that Russians and Ukrainians should make up one people. He schemed for ways to keep Ukraine in Russia's sphere of influence, whether by economic pressure or threats of military force.

Edging Closer to a Crisis

In 2019 the two nations edged even closer to a crisis. Volodymyr Zelenskyy, a comic actor turned grassroots politician, was elected president of Ukraine. One of Zelenskyy's goals was for Ukraine to gain membership in NATO, the military alliance led by the United States. In his view this would secure his nation's pivot to the West and away from Russia and Putin's autocratic ways. But Putin considered such a development completely unacceptable. He swore to prevent it. He had always warned about the dangers to Russia should NATO push eastward to its border. The addition to NATO of Estonia, Latvia, and Lithuania in 2004 had already heightened Putin's concerns. Now he saw the threat increasing day by day. And some experts noted another, perhaps greater worry. "What motivates Putin," says former NATO ambassador Ivo Daalder, "is a concern about the independence of Ukraine — a worry that a functioning, successful, prosperous democracy in Ukraine poses a direct threat to his rule, because it will give people in Russia the idea that they, too, could enjoy what Ukraine enjoys, and rise up against his autocratic rule."[39]

In the spring of 2021, Putin began to mass huge numbers of troops and equipment around Ukraine and in neighboring Belarus. In July Putin published a long article called "On the Historical Unity of Russians and Ukrainians." In it, he repeated his refusal to accept NATO membership for Ukraine. He claimed that the United States and the EU were pushing Ukraine to become a barrier between Europe and Russia. His article concluded with a barely veiled threat: "All the subterfuges associated with the anti-Russia project are clear to us. And we will never allow our historical territories and people close to us living there to be used against Russia. And to those who will undertake such an attempt, I would like to say that this way they will destroy their own country."[40]

In December 2021 US intelligence confirmed that the Kremlin was planning a multifront invasion with more than 175,000 troops. The United States rejected two draft treaties from Russia that both included promises of no NATO membership for Ukraine. American officials warned that an invasion would bring harsh economic sanctions. But President Joe Biden predicted that Russia would invade anyway and suggested that the West's reaction might be muted if it were only a "minor incursion." Zelenskyy's response was swift. "We want to remind the great powers that there are no minor incursions and small nations," he tweeted. "Just as there are no minor casualties and little grief from the loss

> "All the subterfuges associated with the anti-Russia project are clear to us. And we will never allow our historical territories and people close to us living there to be used against Russia."[40]
>
> —Vladimir Putin

of loved ones."[41] Days later Biden stressed that any movement of Russian troops across the border would be considered an invasion. He also declared that Russia would pay a heavy price.

Unleashing Russian Forces

As the world watched anxiously, Putin made his first move. On February 21, 2022, he sent troops into the Russian-controlled areas of the Donbas in eastern Ukraine. He referred to the operation as a peacekeeping mission. Luhansk and Donetsk were recognized by Russia as independent republics with special ties to the Russian Federation. In a rambling and angry televised speech, Putin blamed Ukraine for forcing him to act. Meanwhile, officials in Ukraine and throughout the West condemned Putin's action as a blatant violation of international law.

On February 24 Putin unleashed a full-scale invasion of Ukraine. All at once, Russian forces began pounding cities in central and eastern Ukraine with missiles and artillery fire. Explosions rocked businesses, town squares, and neighborhoods in

Hitting Putin with Sanctions

One of the West's main weapons against Vladimir Putin has been economic sanctions. These are penalties imposed on a nation to stop its aggression or keep it from breaking international law. Sanctions have hit Russia's banking system hard. Its central bank reserves have been frozen, and major Russian banks have been barred from using international payment systems. Russia has defaulted on its debt payments for the first time in more than twenty years. The Russian economy is expected to plunge into a deep recession.

The United States has also tried to hit Putin's oil and gas business, which has helped him finance his war in Ukraine. America has banned all oil imports from Russia. The United Kingdom is phasing out Russian oil imports by the start of 2023.

Sanctions have also targeted more than one thousand Russian individuals and businesses, including Putin himself. Oligarchs close to Putin have had assets frozen and their superyachts seized. In May Britain announced sanctions on Putin's inner circle, including his ex-wife (he was divorced in 2014), his daughters, and his girlfriend, former gymnast Alina Kabaeva. As UK foreign secretary Liz Truss explained, "We are exposing and targeting the shady network propping up Putin's luxury lifestyle and tightening the vice on his inner circle."

Quoted in William Booth, "Britain Places Sanctions on Putin's Alleged Girlfriend, Ex-Wife, Cousins," *Washington Post*, May 13, 2022. www.washingtonpost.com.

an attack reminiscent of World War II in its ferocity. Among the cities targeted were Kyiv, the capital, in the north-central region, and Kharkiv in the northeast.

In an early morning speech on state television, Putin called the invasion a "special military operation." Seated before the Russian flag, he explained, "Its goal is to protect people who have been subjected to bullying and genocide . . . for the last eight years. And for this we will strive for the demilitarization and denazification of Ukraine."[42] Putin ended by repeating his threats against any nation that tried to stop him. As for his claims about genocide and Nazis in Ukraine, they were deliberate lies designed to inflame the Russian public. Although the Ukrainian army contained elements of right-wing militias, Zelenskyy, a Jew, stood as the furthest thing from a Nazi leader.

Western nations condemned the invasion at once. However, to ease fears of a possible world war, the United States announced that it would not respond with military force. Instead, the United States and its allies launched an array of severe economic sanctions on Russian banks, businesses, and oligarchs. But without membership in NATO or any military alliance, Ukraine for now had to defend itself.

A Failed Blitzkrieg

Many observers expected Ukraine to fall to Putin's armies in short order. His apparent strategy was like Hitler's blitzkrieg, or lightning war, in which an adversary is forced to surrender by a speedy and overwhelming barrage of military power. News stories said that the United States offered to help Zelenskyy flee Ukraine and save himself from certain death. Reportedly, he replied, "The fight is here; I need ammunition, not a ride."[43]—a quote that inspired Ukrainians and their supporters everywhere.

As the war continued, Putin's forces met with unexpected resistance. Columns of Russian tanks and transport vehicles became bogged down on the wintry roads, making them easy targets for Ukrainian artillery. Small bands of Ukrainian fighters used knowledge of their home terrain to set up ambushes. The invaders'

In a press conference, Putin called the Ukrainian authorities Nazis and fascists and said his goal in Ukraine is to protect the Russian people who have been subjected to bullying and genocide.

military hardware suffered mechanical failures. Russian soldiers, ordered to attack innocent civilians, experienced sagging morale. When shipments of badly needed high-tech weapons finally arrived from the United States and Europe, Ukrainian defenses became more effective.

Suddenly, military analysts came to a surprising conclusion. Russia had vastly superior forces in manpower and weaponry, but Ukrainians were displaying greater spirit and fortitude in fighting for their homeland. Although Putin claimed that Ukraine was not a real country, Ukrainians were defending it with their lives. Putin's victory was no longer a foregone conclusion. One month after the invasion began, Russian forces still had not captured Kyiv or any other major Ukrainian city.

Nonetheless, the fighting in Ukraine took a heavy toll on both sides. Russia's elite units suffered massive casualties. Millions of Ukrainians fled their homes and escaped to border countries like Poland and Lithuania. Cities such as Mariupol in the south were leveled with shelling. Denied an easy victory, Putin had no intention of pulling back. The initial invasion was hamstrung by flawed planning and intelligence. But he was willing to fight a long war based on Russia's superior artillery and missile capabilities. "Putin most likely also judges that Russia has a greater ability and willingness to endure challenges than his adversaries," said Avril Haines, the US director of national intelligence. "And he is probably counting on U.S. and E.U. resolve to weaken as food shortages, inflation and energy prices get worse."[44]

A Dangerously Unstable Leader

Frustrated by Russia's stalled advance, Putin lashed out at his enemies in the West. At the annual May 9 Victory Day celebration in Moscow's Red Square, he blamed the United States and NATO for the conflict in Ukraine. He claimed once more that Russia was fighting Nazis in Ukraine, just as the Soviet Union had fought Hitler's armies in World War II. Experts on Russia noted signs that Putin was becoming dangerously unstable. Haines told

Putin's Nuclear Threat

Early in his invasion of Ukraine, Vladimir Putin announced that he was putting Russia's nuclear forces on high alert. His threat served to escalate tensions among world leaders and ordinary people like nothing seen since the Cold War. Russia has thousands of nuclear warheads, as does the United States and NATO. Officials in the West condemned Putin's attempt at what they called nuclear blackmail.

But many military experts believe the Kremlin's threats might backfire. They suggest that Putin's allies in China and India would distance themselves should he actually use battlefield nuclear weapons. Moreover, his threats have done more to unify NATO and the West than to sow division. As his tactics in the war have grown increasingly brutal, the United States and NATO countries have ramped up arms shipments to Ukraine's forces despite Putin's nuclear threats. Nonetheless, observers like Daryl Kimball, the executive director of the Arms Control Association, a Washington nonprofit group, urge caution. "I think we need to understand that the risk of miscalculation and escalation is high," says Kimball. "This is a dangerous moment in the crisis. It's a point in which both sides need to back down and move the word 'nuclear' from this equation."

Quoted in Patrick Smith, "Putin Puts Nuclear Deterrent Forces on 'High Alert' Amid Spiraling Tensions over Ukraine," NBC News, February 27, 2022. www.nbcnews.com.

the House Armed Services Committee that he might resort to nuclear weapons if he felt that his regime was in danger of being overthrown. Diplomats like Condoleezza Rice who had dealt with Putin in the past believed he had changed in recent years. Rice said his cold and calculating demeanor had given way to recklessness and delusion.

Western sanctions were taking a sizable bite out of the Russian economy. However, Putin had his own economic weapons, which gave him the potential to spread misery around the world. His disruption of global oil markets contributed to soaring gasoline and food prices in the United States, Canada, and Europe. He threatened to cut off deliveries of natural gas to Germany and other European nations dependent on them. He mined harbors in the Black Sea to cut off massive shipments of Ukrainian grain and fertilizer to markets in North Africa and the Middle East. Economists warned that such measures could spur widespread food shortages, crop failures, and famines. Putin left no doubt that it was all part of a deliberate strategy. He even suggested a kind of food blackmail. He said Russia would have to carefully monitor its own grain exports to countries that were opposed to it. "Russia has a hunger plan," said Yale University historian Timothy Snyder. "Vladimir Putin is preparing to starve much of the developing world as the next stage in his war in Europe."[45]

New Crackdowns and Censorship

Putin's war in Ukraine also brought new crackdowns and media censorship to stifle any opposition. When the invasion began, antiwar protesters had poured into the streets of Moscow and other major cities. During the first two weeks, there were more than thirteen thousand arrests in the peaceful demonstrations. From his prison cell, Putin's foe Alexei Navalny urged Russians everywhere to intensify protests against the war. A message on his Instagram account said, "Mad maniac Putin will most quickly be stopped by the people of Russia now if they oppose the war. You need to go to anti-war rallies every weekend, even if it seems that everyone has either left or got scared. . . . You are the backbone of the movement against war and death."[46]

However, new laws made it a crime to criticize the Russian army or spread information deemed false by Putin, with sentences of up to fifteen years in prison. Police hauled off those with antiwar leaflets or wearing green ribbons, the symbol of resistance to the war. Even state-run media were warned against calling the Ukraine operation a war.

At the same time, Putin made sure the media reports were unfailingly positive. Russian citizens were bombarded with daily stories of military success in Ukraine. They were assured that the main targets of the invasion were Ukrainian Nazis and right-wing militias. Around Moscow, buildings, vehicles, and T-shirts bore the letters Z and V, the symbols of Russia's military invasion. Polls showed support for the war rising to over 80 percent.

"Russia has a hunger plan. Vladimir Putin is preparing to starve much of the developing world as the next stage in his war in Europe."[45]

—Timothy Snyder, historian at Yale University

Ukrainian forces ambush Russian tanks in Kyiv, Ukraine. Analysts noted that while Russia had vastly superior military forces, Ukrainians were displaying greater spirit and fortitude in defending their homeland.

A Bloody Stalemate

As the war in Ukraine dragged on into a bloody stalemate, Putin settled on a strategy of brutal bombardment. He subjected cities in Ukraine to a siege like the one in Leningrad that had maimed his parents' lives. It was also like the destruction of Grozny and Aleppo he had overseen earlier in his career. Whatever the outcome in Ukraine, there was no turning back. He could face judgment for war crimes someday—either from an actual tribunal or from history itself.

Source Notes

Introduction: A Danger to the World

1. Quoted in CBS News, "CBS News Find Evidence of Atrocities Near Ukraine's Capital as Russia Is Accused of War Crimes," April 5, 2022. www.cbsnews.com.
2. Quoted in Roger Cohen, "The Making of Vladimir Putin," *New York Times*, March 26, 2022. www.nytimes.com.
3. Quoted in Steve Gutterman, "'He Has Changed': Putin's Words and Actions Raise Questions About His Rationality," Radio Free Europe/Radio Liberty, February 28, 2022. www.rferl.org.

Chapter One: From the KGB to the Kremlin

4. Quoted in Katie Strick, "Is Vlad Mad or Bad? The Life of Putin—from a Childhood Being Chased by Rats to Today's Isolation and Paranoia," *Evening Standard* (London), March 24, 2022. www.standard.co.uk.
5. Quoted in Masha Gessen, *The Man Without a Face: The Unlikely Rise of Vladimir Putin*. Granta, 2012, pp. 48–49.
6. Quoted in Gessen, *The Man Without a Face*, p. 59.
7. Quoted in Shaun Walker, "How the Soviet Union's Fall Pushed Putin to Try and Recapture Russia's Global Importance," History, February 28, 2022. www.history.com.
8. Fiona Hill and Clifford G. Gaddy, *Mr. Putin: Operative in the Kremlin*. Brookings Institution Press, 2015, p. 10.
9. Quoted in Ksenia Sokolyanskaya, "Putin May Use Chechen War Playbook in Ukraine, Says Russian Human Rights Activist," Radio Free Europe/Radio Liberty, March 6, 2022. www.rferl.org.
10. Quoted in Cohen, "The Making of Vladimir Putin."

Chapter Two: Tightening His Grip on Russia

11. Quoted in Ian Traynor, "Putin Aims *Kursk* Fury at Media," *The Guardian* (Manchester, UK), August 24, 2000. www.theguardian.com.
12. Quoted in Charlie Pittock, "Putin 'Paralysed with Fear' as 2000 Disaster Changed His Approach Forever," Express, April 25, 2022. www.express.co.uk.
13. Quoted in Peter Baker, "Putin Takes Steps to Consolidate His Power," *Washington Post*, September 19, 2004. www.washingtonpost.com.
14. Greg Rosalsky, "How Putin Conquered Russia's Oligarchy," NPR, March 29, 2022. www.npr.org.
15. Quoted in Rosalsky, "How Putin Conquered Russia's Oligarchy."
16. Quoted in Chase Peterson-Withorn, "Oligarch Mikhail Khodorkovsky: 'The World Will Not Be a Safe Place as Long as Putin Remains in Power,'" *Forbes*, May 3, 2022. www.forbes.com.

17. Quoted in Seth Mydans, "As Expected, Putin Easily Wins a Second Term in Russia," *New York Times*, March 15, 2004. www.nytimes.com.
18. Quoted in Rebecca Santana, "Victorious Putin Rejects Criticism of Election," Deutsche Welle, March 15, 2004. www.dw.com.
19. Quoted in Richard Javad Heydarian, "Why Taiwan Is Not the Next Ukraine," Asia Times, February 4, 2022. https://asiatimes.com.

Chapter Three: Silencing Critics and Maintaining Power
20. Quoted in Tom Parfitt, "The Only Good Journalist . . . ," *The Guardian* (Manchester, UK), October 9, 2006. www.theguardian.com.
21. Quoted in B92, "Killed on Putin's Birthday—She Became an Inspiration to Journalists Worldwide," October 7, 2021. www.b92.net.
22. Quoted in Richard Behar, "Another Anniversary of *Forbes* Editor Paul Klebnikov's Unsolved Moscow Murder. (But Rumors of Death of 'Project K' Are Exaggerated.)," *Forbes*, July 14, 2020. www.forbes.com.
23. Quoted in Scott Neuman, "Russia Fatally Poisoned a Prominent Defector in London, a Court Concludes," NPR, September 22, 2021. www.npr.org.
24. Quoted in Deutsche Welle, "Medvedev Wins Election Amid Accusations of Voter Intimidation," March 3, 2008. www.dw.com.
25. Quoted in Gillian Findlay, "Transcript: Putin's Way," *Frontline*, PBS. www.pbs.org.
26. Quoted in Timothy Heritage and Guy Faulconbridge, "Tearful Putin Wins Back Russian Presidency," Reuters, March 3, 2012. www.reuters.com.
27. Quoted in Ellen Barry and Michael Schwirtz, "After Election, Putin Faces Challenges to Legitimacy," *New York Times*, March 5, 2012. www.nytimes.com.
28. Quoted in Sarah Rainsford, "Navalny's Supporters Fear Russia's Putin Wants Him Dead," BBC, April 21, 2021. www.bbc.com.

Chapter Four: Rising Tensions with the West
29. Quoted in Alec Luhn et al., "Edward Snowden Asylum: US 'Disappointed' by Russian Decision," *The Guardian* (Manchester, UK), August 1, 2013. www.theguardian.com.
30. Michael Garcia Bochenek and Kyle Knight, "No Support: Russia's 'Gay Propaganda' Law Imperils LGBT Youth," Human Rights Watch, December 11, 2018. www.hrw.org.
31. Quoted in Reuters, "Russia's Putin Says Liberal Values Are Obsolete: Financial Times," June 27, 2019. www.reuters.com.
32. Quoted in Helier Cheung, "Is Putin Right? Is Liberalism Really Obsolete?," BBC, June 28, 2019. www.bbc.com.
33. Quoted in Cohen, "The Making of Vladimir Putin."
34. Steven Pifer, "Crimea: Six Years After Illegal Annexation," Brookings Institution, March 17, 2020. www.brookings.edu.
35. Quoted in George Packer, "Ukraine Is Redefining America's Interests," *The Atlantic*, February 28, 2022. www.theatlantic.com.
36. Quoted in Natasha Bertrand, "Putin at UN: We Need a 'Genuinely Broad Alliance Against Terrorism, Just Like the One Against Hitler,'" Business Insider, September 28, 2015. www.businessinsider.com.

37. Quoted in Jason Breslow, "Russia Showed Its Playbook in Syria. Here's What It May Mean for Civilians in Ukraine," NPR, March 1, 2022. www.npr.org.
38. Quoted in Owen Dorell, "Russia Engineered Election Hacks and Meddling in Europe," *USA Today*, January 9, 2017. www.usatoday.com.

Chapter Five: Invading Ukraine

39. Quoted in Tucker Reals and Alex Sundby, "Russia's War in Ukraine: How It Came to This," CBS News, March 23, 2022. www.cbsnews.com.
40. Vladimir Putin: "On the Historical Unity of Russians and Ukrainians," President of Russia. https://en.kremlin.ru.
41. Quoted in Mo Abbas, "'There Are No Minor Incursions': Biden's Candid Putin Predictions Criticized in Kyiv," NBC News, January 20, 2022. www.nbcnews .com.
42. Quoted in Andrew Osborn and Polina Nikolskaya, "Russia's Putin Authorises 'Special Military Operation' Against Ukraine," Reuters, February 24, 2022. www .reuters.com.
43. Quoted in Glenn Kessler, "Zelensky's Famous Quote of 'Need Ammo, Not a Ride' Not Easily Confirmed," *Washington Post*, March 6, 2022. www.wash ingtonpost.com.
44. Quoted in Carole Landry, "U.S. Says Putin Is Preparing for a Long War," *New York Times*, May 10, 2022. www.nytimes.com.
45. Quoted in John Haltiwanger, "Putin Is Threatening Poor Countries with Starvation as the 'Next Stage' in His Ruthless Ukraine War, Experts Warn," Business Insider, July 5, 2022. www.businessinsider.com.
46. Quoted in Mark Heinrich, "Jailed Navalny Calls for Anti-War Protests Across Russia on Sunday," Reuters, March 11, 2022. www.reuters.com.

Important Events in the Life of Vladimir Putin

1952   On October 7 Vladimir Vladimirovich Putin is born in Leningrad, the second-largest city in the Soviet Union.

1975   Putin graduates from Leningrad State University and joins the KGB, the Soviet intelligence service.

1983   Putin marries Lyudmila Ocheretnaya after a lengthy courtship.

1985   The KGB assigns Putin to work in Dresden, East Germany.

1991   Putin heads the foreign relations committee of the St. Petersburg mayor's office.

1998   Putin is named director of the Federal Security Service, the agency that succeeds the KGB.

1999   In August Putin is named prime minister of Russia and on December 31 is named acting president; Putin orders a full-scale military assault on rebel territory in Chechnya.

2000   On March 26 Putin is elected to the presidency of the Russian Federation.

2002   Putin orders an assault with poison gas to end a Chechen-led hostage crisis in a Moscow theater.

2003   In October Putin has oil oligarch Mikhail Khodorkovsky arrested and jailed.

2004   Putin does away with elections for leaders in seven federal districts, putting his own handpicked people in charge; Putin easily wins reelection as president, with more than 70 percent of the vote.

2006   Two of Putin's harshest critics, journalist Anna Politkovskaya and former FSB officer Aleksandr Litvinenko, are murdered under mysterious circumstances.

2008   Because of term limit laws, Putin chooses Dmitry Medvedev to run as president while he serves as prime minister for four years.

2012   Putin is elected for his third term as president.

2014   Putin annexes Crimea, a peninsula in southern Ukraine, and sends troops into Ukraine's eastern Donbas region.

2016   Putin authorizes a brutal military assault on Aleppo, a rebel-held city in Syria.

2021   Putin amasses a large number of Russian troops around the border of Ukraine.

2022   Putin orders a full-scale invasion of Ukraine and threatens the use of nuclear weapons.

For Further Research

Books

Anders Aslund, *Russia's Crony Capitalism: The Path from Market Economy to Kleptocracy*. Yale University Press, 2019.

Catherine Belton, *Putin's People: How the KGB Took Back Russia and Then Took on the West*. New York: Picador, 2022.

Bill Browder, *Freezing Order: A True Story of Money Laundering, Murder, and Surviving Vladimir Putin's Wrath*. New York: Simon & Schuster, 2022.

Philip Short, *Putin*. New York: Holt, 2022.

Angela E. Stent, *Putin's World: Russia Against the West and with the Rest*. New York: Twelve/Hachette, 2019.

Internet Sources

Ellen Barry and Michael Schwirtz, "After Election, Putin Faces Challenges to Legitimacy," *New York Times*, March 5, 2021. www.nytimes.com.

Roger Cohen, "The Making of Vladimir Putin," *New York Times*, March 26, 2022. www.nytimes.com.

Paul Kirby, "Why Has Russia Invaded Ukraine and What Does Putin Want?," BBC, May 9, 2022. www.bbc.com.

Tucker Reals and Alex Sundby, "Russia's War in Ukraine: How It Came to This," CBS News, March 23, 2022. www.cbsnews.com.

Andrew Roth, "Putin's Crackdown: How Russia's Journalists Became 'Foreign Agents,'" *The Guardian* (Manchester, UK), September 11, 2021. www.theguardian.com.

Shaun Walker, "How the Soviet Union's Fall Pushed Putin to Try and Recapture Russia's Global Importance," History, February 28, 2022. www.history.com.

Websites

Brookings Institution
www.brookings.edu
The Brookings Institution is a nonprofit public policy organization based in Washington, DC. It conducts in-depth research to help solve problems facing society at the local, national, and global level. Its website features many articles and analyses about Vladimir Putin and his regime.

CIA World Factbook
www.cia.gov/the-world-factbook
This website, which is intended for public use, provides detailed demographic, historic, and cultural information about the countries of the world. Information about Russia and Ukraine can be found by clicking on the "Countries" button at the top of the home page and then using the alphabetical links to the two countries.

Foreign Policy Research Institute
www.fpri.org
The Foreign Policy Research Institute is dedicated to producing the highest-quality scholarship and nonpartisan policy analysis focused on national security challenges that the United States faces. Its website includes articles such as "The Five Lessons That Must Guide U.S. Interactions with Vladimir Putin."

Heritage Foundation
www.heritage.org
The Heritage Foundation's mission is to formulate and promote public policies based on the principles of free enterprise, limited government, individual freedom, traditional American values, and a strong national defense. Its website contains many articles on Vladimir Putin and his strategies in dealing with the West.

Radio Free Europe/Radio Liberty (RFE/RL)
https://pressroom.rferl.org
RFE/RL's mission is to promote democratic values and institutions and advance human rights by reporting the news in countries where a free press is banned by the government or not fully established. It publishes frequent articles and analyses of Vladimir Putin, his regime, and the war in Ukraine.

Vladimir Putin: Russia's Action Man President, BBC
www.bbc.com/news/world-europe-15047823
This website traces the life of Vladimir Putin from birth to the invasion of Ukraine. It provides insight into the man who rules Russia with an iron fist, and includes photographs, a chronology of his life, and links to other articles about Putin.

Wilson Center
www.wilsoncenter.org
The Wilson Center includes the Kennan Institute, a think tank for improving American understanding of Russia, Ukraine, and the surrounding region. The website features frequent blog posts about Putin, the Ukraine war, and Putin's crackdown on media and dissent in Russia.

Index